Sundown At Faith Regional

Also by Barbara Schmitz

How To Get Out of the Body (1999)

How Much Our Dancing Has Improved (2004)

Path of Lightning (Memoir) (2012)

Always the Detail (2014)

What Bob Says Some More (2018)

Just Outside (2019)

Sundown at Faith Regional

Poems by

Barbara Schmitz

PINYON PUBLISHING
Montrose, Colorado

Copyright © 2021 by Barbara Schmitz

All rights reserved. Except as permitted under the U.S. Copyright Act of 1976, no part of this publication may be reproduced, distributed, or transmitted in any form or by any means, or stored in a database or retrieval system, without the prior written permission of the publisher, except for brief quotations in articles, books, and reviews.

Cover Art "Bardo Meditation" by Tremain Smith

Photograph of Makena and Barbara Schmitz by Trisha Schmitz

First Edition: August 2021

Pinyon Publishing
23847 V66 Trail, Montrose, CO 81403
www.pinyon-publishing.com

Library of Congress Control Number: 2021939032
ISBN: 978-1-936671-76-2

ACKNOWLEDGMENTS

"What Do You See Out of the Window You Look Out of the Most" in *Without Fear of Infamy, Scurfpea Poetry Anthology*, 2019

"From Bed" in *Trees in Neighborhood Remember Me, Scurfpea Poetry Anthology*, 2017

"He Knows It's Me" in *Pinyon Review*, Fall 2020

"On the Moon" in *The Briar Cliff Review*, Volume 33, 2021

I would also like to acknowledge Greg Kosmicki and Karen Wingett for reading and editing the manuscript

Suzanne Kehm for terrific technical help and inspiration

Northern Lights Writers for critiquing and suggestions on poems

Susan Entsminger for seeing and choosing these poems.

For Suzanne Kehm and Greg Kosmicki

With gratitude and love.

Contents

Lamentation (After Rumi)   1

CHILDHOOD WINDOWS

White Blossoms   5
Strangers   6
Pain   8
Before   9
Accidental Beauty   11
Childhood Windows   12
Human Relations   13
The Garden   14
Inheritance   15
We Thought   16
"Don't We Look Good in the Pictures No One Took"   19
Father Time   20
Indifference   21

HEART MEDICINE

Heart Medicine   25
The Road   27
We Are Not Arguing   28

Solstice   29
He Knows It's Me   32
Seniors   34
He Called Her   35
If   37
After   39

LOSS

Loss   43
From Bed   45
Give Me Back   46
Flag   48
Might As Well   49
God's Money   50
Winter Solstice   51
Last Page   52
Leaving India   53

OLD DOG

Would You Like?   57
From the Window   58
Dear Insomnia   59
Old Dog   61
All Day She Checks the Boxes   62

Autumn Visit   63
Making the Beds   64
Meditating   66
When God   69
Easy   71
"The Luminous Wind of Morning That Comes Before the Sun"   72
Meditation on Potato Salad   73
Praise   77
On the Moon   79
Worried Again   80
Some Believe   81
House   84
All Night   86
I Believe   87

NOT AFRAID

Not Afraid   91
No Preparation   92
So Sad   93
Sad Songs Sad Stories   94
Last Things   95
Ora Pro Nobis   96
On the Floor   97
To See   98
Consent   99

Autumn Duet   100
"All But a Little of It Blurs and Leaks Away"   101
Days of the Dead   103
When I Am Dead   106
Recompense   108
In My Heaven   109
"To Want Some Things to Live Because They Will
   Live Anyway"   111
"Someone Left the Cake Out in the Rain"   112
Sundown at Faith Regional   113
Nothing at All   114

LAMENTATION (AFTER RUMI)

I thought I could trick Death
by writing poems

Ha! No one wants to read them
when they sail down
from the tower where
Death has flung them

They do not even notice
there are words
on these papers
on which they are blowing their noses

Come, my Love,
we will stand together here
side by side
as long as we can
watching the light

Childhood Windows

WHITE BLOSSOMS

> "We look at the world in childhood.
> The rest is a memory."
> —Louise Glück

She remembers the big-headed peonies
bowing in rain   flushing scarlet in sun

Lake of lily-of-the-valley on
shaded north side of the house

Garden path lined with zinnia guards
big purple dahlias blessing each end

Old chicken coop clubhouse stinking
where the dirty boys were   She didn't
            want in there

Stubby cherry tree she could climb
stubbornly sitting in its crotch
after "The Talk"   *No*

she said to no one mostly herself
I'm not doing that   I'm not bleeding
White blossoms not yet turned
            into deep red fruit

Reading *Gone with the Wind* she
sat on a bee but there were fireflies
            that night

and pinwheels spinning sparks
into sky on the 4th of July

STRANGERS

> "We could be two strangers
> thrown together by chance"
> —Jack Gilbert

Someone plucked us up
        young   beautiful
        both in cut-off shorts
       shapely legs
dropped us here
where we slept for more than
                            fifty years
to awaken today
cool breezy day in summer

We've slept so long we have creases
      up and down thighs
      on faces next to eyes
One of us has a loose tooth
The other not any

The vines and trees
    very green
    and waving

Someone has done a pretty good job
                      on the flower garden
Bright pink red and orange zinnias
honeysuckle
ordinary but plentiful day lilies

Trucks full of chapters of our lives
we must have lived through
        but forgotten somehow
rumble on by
        down the highway
        swiftly now
                disappearing with
                        far away train whistle

PAIN

> "We are all human.
> We protect ourselves the best we can"
> —Louise Glück

not lying exactly
but stretching the truth
with our arms so
        it fits over our shoulders

Our shoulders broad
for a female   Long arms
and legs for a girl born
in those days

Those days when girls weren't
taught to catch a ball   to
step up to the bat
        what the bleeding was for

The bleeding was to continue
life   We didn't know
        how to seek pleasure

so we sunk back   built
fantasy towers and daydream lakes
looking to our souls for answers
        forgetting we had bodies

BEFORE

The night before I started high school
still faint farewell light in evening sky
I had taken my bath
washed my hair
      finally learning how to roll it
      on brush rollers

Parents drive Dad's red mercury
      into garage
coming home from grandparent's
where Dad did house maintenance
worked on their temperamental well

Looking out bedroom window
too early to go to sleep
teetering on the edge
      of the unknown

Tomorrow I would begin
      my walk away
      from this house
      Dad had remodeled

Up the hill to high school
      (I could walk
      even in deep snow)

For a while glancing back
      to make sure they
      were still there
           snug in the front seat
They always returning

while my orbit around them
widened and widened
      into outer space

ACCIDENTAL BEAUTY

Sometimes you don't
even know

If your mother
didn't know

and didn't
dress you so

Sometimes
it's not until a boy
comes along   smiling
and kissing and trying
to slip his hand inside
your clothes

Suddenly
like a thwack in head
you say *He must think
I'm pretty*

CHILDHOOD WINDOWS

By the windows I knew North   looking
out living room panes beside the TV
toward father's huge garden

That was the way to Omaha
big city where I was born
where mother birthed me in labor room
Father home from hunting pheasants

She got lost in Omaha   first time
away from home   gone for a job

She went back to her tiny town
staying there safe in her pumpkin house
cooking and canning   Never did
she learn to swim   Me neither

HUMAN RELATIONS

No one was allowed anger in my house
                      except my father
He didn't strike but noisy bluster
                      and loud ranting scared us
Whittled down we needed less space

Mother whined
            cajoled
            repeated her complaints
            endless uncoiling ribbon

Brothers pounced and pounded
                boofed and popped
      BB guns   slingshots
              cherry bombs

Tiptoed to my closet
            I daydreamed
                    living library stories
              Emerging   cautious rabbit
            only when made to do dishes

THE GARDEN

    (for Robin)

Robin and I had a garden
It was at her house
She set the strings
        to make straight rows
It was my idea to bless
        the ground with beer
She must have pulled the weeds

My son was small and liked
        to tend the garden
We mostly ate the peas
        and some of the beans raw
Sometimes I declined to drive
        way across town to retrieve
            a tomato

Now the garden's just a butterfly flicker
        flashing in my mind
leaving us laughing in deep green grass
with little black dog Sparky

INHERITANCE

Our fathers
and mothers
creep
into our bodies
when we
are young
and napping

they stretch
out their legs
and hands
inside us
and hang on
tight all

through our
days and
long nights
nodding
at what
they like

reaching
out for
their favorite
things holding
us back

when we get
close to anything
that smells
like what
they fear

WE THOUGHT

We thought
we would ride
bikes
Seemed like a sane
fairly safe
even enjoyable
activity for two
nose-in-books
people

We bought the best—
Gitane racing bikes
This was before
mountain bikes with
big tires
before most other
folks rode bikes

We did ride
a little around close-by
neighborhoods
All the while
I imagined I would do
a marathon
would do one of those
colossal
bike rides
with many people
over several days

I could do it
if I wanted I reasoned
I still think
I could have
but my partner
not so inclined

I did ride
to my teaching job
a few times
but arrived sweaty
one time with seat
split
out of my pants

One time
a guy reached out
his window
whapped me
on the butt
nearly crashed me
into the gulch

We had a secret
meeting place
when we rode together
almost
any place
Pedaled to
a quiet spot
edged close

legs and bikes
balanced
kissed sweetly
tenderly

Probably why
we bought
the bikes anyway

"DON'T WE LOOK GOOD IN THE PICTURES NO ONE TOOK"

—Lawrence Raab

We didn't have a camera
We didn't bother
We were out of film
It was too much trouble
We were having too much
      fun to stop to pose
It was scary and shaky on top
      the Ferris wheel
We were late for a meal
We thought we needed makeup
We didn't know
      we were young
      we were gorgeous
We didn't believe in Time's river
We didn't know about gathering
        rosebuds
We were full of hope
We seldom thought of
      ailments
      age
      inevitability
No one wants to see your
        vacation photos

FATHER TIME

Father Time lugs his night sack
      of leftover dreams
      and cookie crumbs
      into morning kitchen

Leaving go of his burden
He straightens his back
so I can see eyelight twinkle

Ah!
He reminds me of someone
I knew once
long long ago

INDIFFERENCE

Black chair
always
it seems
been here

Gathering
outside light
onto
its shoulders

Reading
the air
and tempo
of the day
while turned away

Tuned to
our interior
Not attached
to external

Remembers
(maybe)
We/it
were happy

No intention
to record
or horde

just witness
the passing

Heart Medicine

HEART MEDICINE

It's medium leakage
        says the nurse practitioner
        about husband's heart
        pointing to the upper chamber
        of a heart pasted to the wall
            at cardiac doctor

There's mild and extreme she
        goes on matter-of-factly
so we're adding more blood pressure
        medicine
Since you're already at maximum dose
        on your current blood pressure pill
        we're giving you another

I nod
        That'll make 24 daily medications
            I think
        divided into a two-part bag
            morning and night
Pretty good about taking them
        I mentally note
    Although at night I have to ask
        a time or two
        Did you take your medication?

Easier for me than Ritalin
        which sometimes I put
        in his hand in the morning
        and he's still holding
            when I return from the kitchen

If he remembers to take it
    by 1:30 in afternoon
    he can usually swallow supper
Sometimes if I'm leaving
    I set the timer

Yet he waltzes through his days
    like the amazing young man
        I met in college
    skipping class and staying home
    to breathe in the beauty
of the leaves transforming
    into red and gold

THE ROAD

Car on bumpy country highway
Stop light on roadwork bridge
Round hay bales still in field

To doctor in Omaha for him today
Doctor at home for me in two days
He preparing for surgery   Me

waiting for lab news after
surgery two days before
Easter over   Bird Egg sky

Trees poke leafy fingers into air
Monster dump truck snorts
jake brakes shoving us along
                             from behind

Youth zooms by in black Mustang
convertible   top down
grinning   and waving

WE ARE NOT ARGUING

but when he issues an opinion
      I think it over
         and present other facets
Have you thought of it this way?

You disagree with everything I say

No, I don't

I don't get any support for my ideas

Can't you see me nodding?
        I'm just expanding the discussion

It's our system
We've set ourselves up to disagree

I don't agree with that!

SOLSTICE

It is Jean's birthday
I call her but she's
not home Seems to
have no answering machine

We all used to go somewhere
two and one-half hours
before sunrise to chant
the Kundalini mantra ECK ONG KAR
SAT NAM   SIRI WA GURU

You're supposed to
get enlightened if you
do it
        Husband and I've chanted on mountains,
        in farm fields   on our house
        roof with babe in arms

We no longer
        get up in the summer dark
        or go anywhere
        or chant much
                maybe a little
                here and there
                throughout the day

ECK ON KAR   SAT NAM
        SIRI WA GURU
We've both had surgeries
        He's not getting better
Cat scan finds something else

Workers come to mow the lawn
Eric's so tall he can nod at me
over six-foot fence as I chop off
wilted daisies When he starts
the weed eater it sings
QUACK QUACK QUACK
like my granddaughter's toy duck
she chases us with
If she were here she'd yell
   WHAT'S THAT NOISE?
and run to see
like the noise from the trucks
     and motorcycles on Highway 81
WHAT'S THAT NOISE?

WHAT'S THAT NOISE? She jumps up
   almost asleep after fourteen stories
   when our anniversary clock chimes

WHAT'S THAT NOISE? I shout
going down to check the laundry
and hear water gushing—
the extension on the hose
  for automatic watering
  has blown off
and water floods from outside
   down the basement walls

ECK ONG KAR
        I was going to call Jean back
SAT NAM
        I thought I'd surely be
                enlightened by now
SIRI WA GURU

HE KNOWS IT'S ME

He knows it's me he says
although he's toward the back
in this upstairs apartment/house
of the widow of the Head of the Whirling Dervish

We've left our shoes downstairs
women covered their heads and
eaten our piece of hard candy we
each selected from a passed-around dish

She holds the hand of our guide's wife
staring at her nails and babbling
Later we learn the widow's told her
she won't be able to have a good meditation
if she wears nail polish

We've also passed around her husband's beads
Everyone touches them   So why are we so
busted-heart joyful about prayer beads I
wonder and who is this old grandma
with a babushka anyway? She says she
misses God but will be with him soon

The wailing spirals up and out of my soul
leaving my mouth as I watch its misery-
trail like the energy off the fingers of the
Dervish Whirlers, Turners   It is not quiet
crying but sobby hiccoughs An ancient
archetypal grief of humanity triggered
by our earlier argument about how my
husband is spending money My worry
of having enough to carry us safely home

He's thrown money at me threatened to
break his glasses and now it's not just our
puny bickering but tears of sorrow of God's
whole creation   longing and loss   and
out-of-control spinning of our lives
on this whirling planet and how all
of us must do our dance of suffering

When he looks around he finds it's
indeed me, my crying   And he doesn't
have to fix me, fix anything   because
now my head is in the widow's lap   She's
stroking my hair cooing   Loving us all—
all of us her children   Babies she'll carry
along when she gets at last to see
God face to face

SENIORS

Is today Saturday? he'll ask
I usually know and can answer
It's those other questions
      the name of So-and-So
      or the talk at such-and-such occasion
Given his lengthy description
I almost always know what he means
      but as soon as he asks
      some over-zealous teacher's pet
      leaps up erasing the blackboard
          of my mind

Then sometime later in the day
      the person's name
      the event in question
pops right out of my mouth
          out loud
while I'm at the sink
or sweeping up walnuts
      astonishing
      effortless

HE CALLED HER

He called her Pinky
She called him Putums

He called her Morning Star
She called him Night Light
Good Time   Piano Man
Bright Dancer

He called her Mother of my Child
She called him Daddy Lion
growling and stalking on his knees
as she fed baby at her breast

She said she liked him best
He said he liked her better
than anybody

He called her Stubborn
She called him Frivolous

When she gave him his morning's
bowl of yogurt he said
she was nice

She said he was kind to
explain the stereo over and over

He said it was all right when she
blew out the speakers
She said it didn't matter when
he ran into the curb

She asked what he wanted for dinner
He said he didn't know

What do you want to do? he asks
What do you want to do? she echoes

IF

If you were tall
        I'd want to be taller still
more skinny
so like a lanky sister tree
I could plop sweet cherries
        or sour lemons
onto your noggin
trying to knock some sense
        into your so-in-love-with-the world
                whistle
        and don't-you-believe-everybody's-good
                lyrics
catch a couple of the handouts you toss
        to everyone at large
        deserving and undeserving
                lives and lies

I'd be your crabby school marm
        making you stay in at recess
        writing over and over until
        you disappear in a cloud of chalk
EVIL DOES EXIST
        But once released into the street
        You'd yell *Why think about it all the time?*

I'd rewrite your slap-dash happy endings
        with some reality grammar
                red pen marking
Leaving you some margin notes
We are not only here to have fun
Not everyone can play all the time

I'd put you on display in
        a glassed museum case
Here is a man
who believes in beauty
believes the sun forevermore rises
thinks there are better things to
        occupy our minds
than sorrow   like jelly beans

I would be the corner display
dressed in silk and linen
with Dylan's ballad *Sad-Eyed Lady of the Lowlands*
        reeling out over these scenes
these you's
these me's

AFTER

After reflection of aspen trees
        floats like white clouds
        over our blue-sky lives
passing and gone in van windshield

After the day on acid
      (me)
Peyote   (friends)
Ankle-deep in icy stream

We come down
      from the mountain
Hungry as our wild souls
Unable to agree on food

Bean burritos in fast-food parking lot
      tasty as Sweden and the Nobel Prize

Loss

LOSS

When it comes down to it   it's
all loss   We buy and buy
Accumulate   art   books
clothes   cars   appliances   friends
Then they wear out   get misplaced
get boring   No longer bring thrills
or even joy   We get more   Try
harder   Buy bigger   better   while
a funny little rabbit in a magician's
hat   keeps grabbing things   denting
them with hammers   spilling juice
on our treasured cashmere sweater
A stain that can't be removed

We can try to be like Thoreau
Simplify Simplify   Move to
Walden Pond   But there are not
enough ponds for everybody
and besides he only lived there
a couple years and probably
went there because the woman
he wanted turned him down and
married his brother

Lost loves?   Do you know where
your first love is?   Do you care?
Would you want to see a photo
of him now?   In the *Alexandrian
Quartet* the narrator finally met
his love again after many years
She was marred by smallpox
and had grown fat

St. Francis threw his father's fabrics
from the tower chanting *Give it
all away, Father It won't make
you happy* and met the Pope as
a poor monk   His Holiness in jewel-
encrusted crown and rich robes
was not eager for Francis' message

FROM BED

Ring around full moon
shining through paneled
                bay window

Can't believe Day Lilies
           Star of Bethlehem
           Peonies
are pulling themselves up
           on their elbows
heads up into air Still cold
           Bitey wind

Can't believe it's cancer
        Not me
        I won't get it!

Bow says the breeze
Open arms hums the moon

GIVE ME BACK

give me back the time before
worry   just do and did and
think about consequences later

take away *yes but's* and *what if's*
the time machine projection
of future catastrophes

give me no more symptoms,
procedures, take-as-directed
medication for all the ailments
that keep squeezing themselves
into the short segment remaining

give me glittering even on moonless
nights   glitter they say has something
to do with genius   inspiration

give me inspiration the in-breath
one more noseful   mouthful
lung full of air   light

eyes alight give me wonder
breathing into a recipe stirring
up something that through
alchemy becomes bodies

lighting faces   lighting fires
like father burning raked leaves
in the barrel next to the alley
next to the lilac bush the old
chicken coop which smelled
forever of feathers and poop
but brothers made into a clubhouse

take away smoke in her nostrils
what could it mean? is it from
some medication she takes   burning
bridges until the only way is
forward   then where?

maybe oblivion   having to choose
old hotel with glass ceiling
bathroom down the hall or
fifties motel run by Indian family
with shrines to Sarasvati and Shiva
at the check-in desk

old building with ghostly
murmurings of sexual embraces
sighs and moans   erotic replay
of lifetimes past

FLAG

Friend wants me to get a pole or rod
something long enough to reach
the tattered clear plastic bag
snared by the backyard maple—

whipping and snapping
down-right carrying on
from it high-up post—
overlooking yard, highway, everybody's

business. It flutters so
obstinately there, convincing
me that it is necessary
to this scene, this life of mine.

I shake my head, *You like it?*
he asks. *Yeah,* I say, *like
the runt of the litter, moth-eaten
childhood toy. Let it fly*

its no color, rippled ripple.
Beauty waves its peculiar flag
capturing odd worshipers.

MIGHT AS WELL

> "This is no joke.
> That's what makes it funny."
> —Leonard Cohen

We might as well laugh
as we *ashes ashes*
all fall down Towers
falling on our heads
Bridges collapsing *O*
where O where has my
little dog gone?

To the other side gently
We will miss him
Fur and fluffy sweetness
So try the laughing yoga
pose   HO-HO-HO from
deep belly   Maybe

the sun will come out
and sparkle the snow
before grey skies clinch
their teeth and let go with

more white fury *You've*
got to accentuate the positive
Everyone knows Pollyanna
turned out all right   Peering
into deepest night   Could
that be the tiniest of light
    cracking Dawn's egg
    all yellow and runny?

GOD'S MONEY

The woman in Jerusalem begging at the Wailing Wall
screamed at me, *This is what you give me?*
Being confused as usual about money, especially
foreign bills, I had handed her my smallest. I thought
first to apologize but she squawked, hands on her hips,
and turned away. Then considered retrieving it
but turned as well. I had come to see The Wall—
having had to go in through the women's door to
the women's section. All the rabbis in tiny hats,
curls, and cords wound around their arms—
What did it mean?

I touched the wall, trying to see what I
could feel and forget about the money
and also the one man who had jumped
before our group the day before. *You
are from America?* We nodded. *Give
me money!* Our guide declined.

Standing there I remembered the other
man with a black nose in Kashmir who
would not allow us women into the mosque.
When we turned to leave, he held up
his jar, yelling, *You give a donation!*

At Moinuddin Chisti's tomb in Ajmer
at a special ceremony for men only,
my husband felt someone reach
into his pocket for his wallet.

WINTER SOLSTICE

It's like New Year's says Husband
on this shortest day/longest night
Humans have dreamed all
these festivities
to keep the gloom away
tinsel candles cookies and wine

We celebrate being alive
Friend's husband died yesterday
Doctor cut time from my face

Sorrow and joy equally stacked
wrapped in paper shining
beneath star-topped tree

Let it all begin again   continue
Leaky hearts keeping time
in this breathe-breathe life
we've come to

stepped down from angelic ladders
to live here and sing
have coffee with cream   sliced pears

LAST PAGE

> "the last page of
> the book of summer"
>   —George Bilgere

comes before autumn's tricky
beauty designed to sneak
winter onto the scene while
we're gaping at gold and flaming red

no one tries to argue
with winter's gravity just
hunker down in caves which
occasionally allow a glimpse
of bright sky through thin-wall cracks

spring's another whole story
we weren't sure we'd find
on Life's library shelf
we clink our glasses, shake
our heads, mumble incantatory
              thank you's

while we amble toward blissful
air   that full-blown season
we are sure this time will
last forever

LEAVING INDIA

The guy at the Delhi Airport
strikes up a conversation
as we're lying in reclining

chairs trying to at last rest,
waiting to go through security,
again! (They'll want me

to give up my potato
chips I just bought but
relent when I squawk).

He sells farm machines,
*What are you doing in
India?* I ask. His eyes

flash. *Donating,* he answers.
I look puzzled. *Sperm!* he
announces. *I'm a sperm

donor.* I want to ask,
India needs more sperm?
but don't and he goes

on about how much
money he's getting—Indian
women want to have

babies with white men.
Oh India! You've surprised
me again—your hustle, hordes

your quirky perspectives.

Old Dog

WOULD YOU LIKE?

Would you like to have a colonoscopy
 on Valentine's Day? the nurse asks
  calendar in her hand

Head tilted to the side I want to ask,
 Would you?
but instead play it like Bartleby, the Scrivener,
 replying, *I'd prefer not to*

I tell FIXNOW who calls six or seven
 times a day
to call no more
We want nothing they are selling
This is harassment
I'm going to report them
 (to whom I wonder?)
but they call a couple more times

Good place I decide to let fly
 resentments, anger, stress
but all those menacing birds turn
back loose on me   fluttering flapping
round about my head and heart

I search my closet-heart-chest
for my Indifference Cloak
turns me into a Superhero
 imperturbable
if only I remember
 to put it on

FROM THE WINDOW

There she blows   Old Friend
Old-Lady-Like-Me   Walnut Tree

I didn't feel old until lately
This year she makes few walnuts

Are her leaves sort of yellow?
Should I let my hair turn grey?

Can't we all just go along
acting as if everything's okay?

DEAR INSOMNIA

I never wished to make your acquaintance
I do not know you as a friend
    I'd prefer
    to keep eyes squinched tightly
    hoping you'll go on your way
    let me be
        even weaving through
        the maze of a bad dream
        if it's not too scary
I'd still be here when I awake

When I'm awake
    through these long blank hours
    I do not feel your sympathy
    you do not reach for my hand
Sometimes you break loose
    a fragment of your meanness
    and send it flapping about
    the black night
    on bat wing
        swooping around my head

Insomnia, how can we solve this problem?
    Not a pill taker
    I sprinkle herbs into nighttime routine
    Flip pillow over
        to produce cooler head rest
Flop body this side
        that way
Get up for a drink
Stumble
    More awake now that ever

I'd like to make a plan, Insomnia
        Could you cut me a break
                now and then?
So I could arise
        bright-eyed and bouncy
not dragging tired horse
            through duties and days

How about an armistice?
I could attest to your power
Pay tribute to your terrible capacity
        to hold hostages for nights
                      on end

Insomnia, I'm praying for you
        I'm pleading with you
Insomnia, what are we going to do?
Insomnia, are you listening to me?

OLD DOG

She is trying to learn
        a new trick
              sleeping on her back
                      Not much progress

When knees ache
        painful joints
she can tuck a pillow
        under her legs
rest there   a while

But unlike all curled up
        protected
        on one side
        or the other

back sleeping's the position
        where ghouls and ghosts
        can snatch and touch
vulnerable to spirit's breath

Night hours take their time
strolling along with her mind
On her back she keeps practicing

Woof

ALL DAY SHE CHECKS THE BOXES

Like X
Dislike X
everything she sees

It's like a Facebook quiz:
        Do you like this red?
        How about this blue?

The wings to the heart Sufis say
        are independence
        and indifference

Will she ever become neutral?
        Too much eyeliner on hospital receptionist
False eyelashes too much
        Neighbor's hay bale, cornhusks
            scarecrow decorations corny
        Also animated Leonard Cohen video—
            his spirit flying over Montreal

There are some likes
        Patch of yellow in green maple leaves
        Zinnias waving in driveway garden

Mostly she dislikes/likes
        her way all through the day
        on upstairs to bed
where mattress is too warm
but she likes the paintings

AUTUMN VISIT

So many body parts
for things to go wrong,
I say to my hair stylist
who says lately her shoulder's
been okay but now it's
her hip and leg hurting.

Ai. I say, and then there are
all the squishing, pumping,
chugging internal organs
not to mention the teeth.
a dull ache which persists
on my upper left side.

We laugh. We hug. She
mixes many shades
of red to color my
aging head. *Vibrant!*
she exclaims, *like an*
Autumn leaf!

I nod not mentioning
the last blaze
before the ending.

MAKING THE BEDS

Hardly ever do I not
                do it

(Only sometimes to have
       husband turn covers down
       an hour or two later for
              a nap)

I do it over and over
like rinsing dishes for machine
folding handkerchiefs
      (lots of those
        mate's got a perpetual
              runny nose)

I always wondered what
      "perpetual light" was
that was supposed to "shine
      upon them"

That prayer the priest intones
      at funeral masses
where hardly anything is mentioned
      about the loves and joys
      of the deceased
just mumblings and hopes
mainly about eternity
      which is already now happening
      but most of the time
we don't notice

just go about our busy busyness
        buying stamps
        arranging the magazines
            tossing a few away
        fretting about recycling

Prayers we could be making
        out of the mundane

MEDITATING

I have learned to meditate
        kind of
        sort of
I mean I know the techniques
        I'm supposed to sit up
        straight
(real form is cross-legged)
        but a chair will do
tuck your chin in
        (gets a little more complicated
        as you get older)
hands on knees
or in a mudra   a ritual form
        for your hands like tai chi for the body

They say when Lou Reed died he just
        did the tai chi movements in the air
        with his beautiful musician hands

Ginsberg sang a song about meditation
        accompanying himself with his harmonium
Sit you sit down
Tell the Super Powers to sit and meditate
Lie down you lie down
Eat when you eat
Die when you die
Die when you die

Eckhart Tolle says *No thinking*
    Just look at the flower
    Be with the flower
    Don't say   *I want that flower*
for my garden

He would say
    we must drop our Pain Body
    an entity of accumulated pain
    and justifications that makes us
    continue to suffer and stay in
    our misery

So sit
    Be still and know that I am God
    the Bible says   Joe Miller says
We can get it if we get
    still enough

The thought that comes through my body
makes me move   *I think therefore*
I move

Then I remember I'm supposed to be
meditating

In TM we went back to the breath
        Did you have any thoughts? asked
        the teacher. *I did,* I replied
        Then just return to your breath,
        she smiled

Jack Kornfield laughed at me at
the Seven-Day Retreat in silence
I did with Natalie Goldberg at
Lama Mountain. Angry and aching
when I finally got an interview, I said
        I came here to know God and all
        I'm doing is sitting here watching
        my breath! All the teachers giggled

What do you think God is, he said

WHEN GOD

I try to stay awake at night
      this time of my life
      any time in my life

Mother trained me to go to bed at 9
Czech grandma said *When God turns*
      off the light you go to sleep

People naturally went to sleep
about 8:30 spiritual teacher says
Got up at 4

      if I lived alone
      if I lived in a cloister

I'd love to go into the other world
      early evening
      about when the birds are fluttering
      bickering   trying to find
      the right spot   safe and
                        comfortable
perfect tree top
      to back into
      sail down upon

Traveling when Twilight begins
to lower her darkling skirt
      a feeling aches in stomach pit
Where will we sleep?
When can we stop?

When can we settle into soft beds
away from the menacing stars?

quiet earth
tigers lions sleeping
ancient gods at rest
secrets safe

EASY

to bend to pain in the gut
to forget to look up
        rinsed May sky   shining
        you've planted some zinnias
                bachelor buttons
                    cosmos
        maybe they'll sprout
        maybe the mole
                vole
        living below will find another yard

There has been a prediction
All will be well

no definite time for everything
        to step into its proper position
        for stomach cramps to stop
        for the swollen river to subside

nothing can return the way
        it was before
but maybe there'll be some sandy beaches

maybe old letters found in a drawer
will uncode some of the puzzling mystery

why our lives veered this way
        instead of that

"THE LUMINOUS WIND OF MORNING THAT COMES BEFORE THE SUN"

—Mark Strand

The last dreams before the eyes
are pried open by light are the events
that haven't happened yet

Lovely gifts and small disasters
wait just over the close-up hilltop
like guests at the surprise party

who pop up, sing, or scream
delighting or terrifying the unknowing
recipient who like all of us reaps

her just and unjust deserts

MEDITATION ON POTATO SALAD

    (for Doug Kuper)

Favorite food
    used to be my mother's
    She 20 years gone
    leaving no recipe

Now Doug Kuper's
    from Kuper Farm Store
    makes it himself
    I don't know how
    but it's better than I
    remember my mother's
    usually the long-gone-food
    is remembered as better tasting
        deeper
        fresher
        more juicy

but his:
    potatoes, salad dressing, eggs, onion
    sugar, evaporated milk, mustard, salt
wins the Oscar!

I try not to buy it
because rarely can I stop
and not eat the whole container
so I buy the smallest size
put it way back in the fridge
try to forget I have it

until in the morning kitchen
turning on the light
memory flashes on
Potato Salad!
      checking the clock
      I see it's 10:30
It could be an early lunch
I carefully take
          not-quite-half
spoon it into another dish

drop some on the knives
      in open silver wear drawer
      have to wash and dry four knives
take bowl to favorite living room chair
      Begin
      Then remember Seven-Day-Meditation Retreat
          in silence on Lama Mountain

We were required to meditate even
      when we ate
Pick up fork
Pick up food with fork
Bring fork to mouth with bite of food
Place food in mouth
Chew
Chew
    Taste
Swallow
      noticing the whole process
      all the while

so painful it took usually
    45 minutes to an hour
    to finish lunch

Lift fork
Put food in mouth
Chew
Chew Taste
Swallow
    each bite
    each bit of food

On the last day when
they let us talk at lunch
    I found I could not
        talk and eat
            at the same time
        ended up spitting food
            on meal mates

I begin
    Lift
    Chew
        Taste
        Swallow

When I think of Meditation
            Retreat
I forget potato salad
even though I am eating it

If my food is something like
    potato salad
I usually try to eat it all
    quickly
so I don't have to keep
    thinking about it
    in the refrigerator
    for the rest of the day

It's gone!
It's over!
    No more thought of resisting
        or planning
    when I deserve to
        go eat the rest

I look in my bowl
    It's empty
Ah! I can still lick it out
which I do
    mmmmm!   delicious
then take it
    to the dishwasher
remembering I almost made it
    out of the store
    without buying any

PRAISE

Praise be to Thee, Neighbor's
        Evergreen tree
           bowing and shivering
all these years performing grace

Praise be for grace of morning
          to be alive again
              to have no stomach ache
                headache
sun with clouds

Praise be clouds that chase
            sun away
that carry rain's kiss
to water all we've planted
        not yet planted

Praise be flowers not yet planted
        roots not yet clasped to earth
        not yet sunk into the cycle
        of air-light-rain-blossom
            unfurl and shine

Praise be unfurl and shine
        pink magenta purple
            yellow splash
                accent of red

Praise be red
        birth   death
part of the heart

Praise the heart
>that beats and flutters
>that breathes
>>sees and waits

Praise the waiting
>the watching and knowing
>all the hum
>>everything
>>going about its business

lawn mower   cars   street sweeper
>tick tock clock
>baby wailing
Happy Birthday song

Praise the Praise Song
>Thankful for blessing
>Thankful for pain
>>for statue of St. Michael
>>guarding the garden
>>(with a hollow in his heart)
>>bestowing benediction
>>grass   weed   rock

ON THE MOON

    (for Marge)

A day on the moon
       is two weeks long
That means
       the nights are too

Bad news for insomniacs
       but owls
       night lifers
            booze hounds
            and prowlers
                  get bonuses

And Oh! La-de-da
       the hookers rake
       in the dough for two weeks
       get loaded and sleep it off
            for two

Nightmares gather their forces
       lift weights to build strength
            for such long-session hauntings

And dreams dally and dance
       braid flowers through their hair
       that'll never ever last until morning

WORRIED AGAIN

> "… worried again about the hopelessness
> of worry"
> —Lawrence Raab

It is only a habit
spiritual teacher explains
      patient as always

and although I know
      this must be so
it's hard to stare down
      the clattering brain

get ahold of it
      caw   caw
long enough to give it
      a good talking to

to promise rewards
if it stops all that imagining
      of catastrophes
(positive reinforcement *must* work)

First you must get brain's
      attention
and then speak to it
      rather loudly
even though it won't admit it
      brain is very hard-of-hearing

SOME BELIEVE

They believe power lines in the trees started
the California fires
The power company believes they shouldn't
have to pay for it this time
Rudy Giuliani believes the truth isn't the truth
Donald Trump believes everything uttered
from his lips and fingers
Press Secretary doesn't believe it but she
says it anyway
The News doesn't believe it's fake
My granddaughter believes there are people
on top of her swing set
Some believe it's all a conspiracy
        Kennedy assassination
        9/11
or a fake
        Moon Landing
Some believe in aliens
        the good grey kind
Some believe in shaman
Some believe in priests
Some believe the priests should be punished
        for their abuses
Ronald Regan's son Ron does not believe
        in God
Some still believe Obama wasn't born
        in America
Some believe America is great
Some believe it never was great
Some believe it can be great again

Some believe in the flag
Some believe in not standing for the National Anthem
Some believe if they are football players
    they should be fired
Some believe in Fatima
Some believe they saw Mary's face
    in a tortilla

Some believe in Heaven
One Pope said there is no Hell
Some believe an unbaptized soul
    will go to Limbo
Some believe in the healing powers
    of the holy dirt from the Sanctuario
    in New Mexico
Some refuse to believe in Global Warming
Some believe in their doctors
Some do not believe in any doctors
Some like vitamins
Some really like this Pope
Some believe in Capital Punishment
Some believe abortion is wrong
Some believe we must give money
    to anyone who asks
Some have faith in God
Carl Jung said, "First you must experience
    then you can believe"
Some believe in money
Some believe in love
Some believe they will not die
Everyone eventually believes they will die

Some believe they will be Raptured
    if they believe
Some believe their bones and ashes
    will rise up when Jesus comes at last

HOUSE

sings
its own
midnight song

Pop
Creak
Moan

Could be
someone
walking

around
upstairs
but it's

only
house
sighing

letting go
of its
dust

of days
everybody's
business

Noisy
Quiet
Finally it

breathes itself
la la
deep

back
to origin
of beginning

ALL NIGHT

> "The trees stand all night
> every night of their lives"
> —Marge Saiser

Oh! what woe to never recline
never to be horizontal
        after holding yourself up all day
no rest after supper   dishes done
not to have a soft
            or even semi-hard
                    pillow under hear

to have no one
        tug the covers up
no bedtime story
no prayers
            (well maybe there are
            some soft mumblings
            of oneness with sky
            and birds)

no goodnight kiss
no one turning off the moon
        or the partying stars
        laughing and bouncing
        around the sky

to have no loved one say
Good night, Sweetheart,
        See you in the morning

I BELIEVE

I believe that Walgreens has a right be next door
on the corner with its all night lights and all day
parking lot. I believe I have learned to love its
cursive red title scrawled across its white front and
facade with lit up mortar and pestle. I believe I
have come to like its smiley-faced pharmacists who
do try to get me discounts and explain what
I need to know about my medication.

I believe Highway 81 has a right to flow, zoom,
beep, and honk past my house but the crotch rockets
should have their tires shot off for deliberately farting
their obnoxious booms into spring and summer night sky.

I believe in God, not the Father Almighty, maybe the
Son and Holy Ghost. The Holy Ghost used to haunt
my closet when I was a tiny girl. I don't believe in
Heaven except for the Heaven of Sweet Breath, knowing
I am not my body but something else inside who doesn't
die, disappear or go away,

I believe in young love that's stupid and naïve and
learns to grow big and old and patient and kind.

Eyes that smile, kiss, radiate the soul through
from the other side.

I believe in Please and Thank You and What Can I Do For You?
Lilacs, peonies, and the smell of the ground in spring
before the grass wakes up.

I believe in voices that don't grow old that you can always recognize.

The smell of my grandmother I'll always remember.

Chili bubbling. The morning sky just before dawn.

How come we get this chance to eat and laugh
and leave it all behind?

I believe we are lucky.

Not Afraid

NOT AFRAID

I'm not afraid to die
he said at the hospital
when he could still talk

Before he pulled the blanket
over his head when we
went for a birthday visit

Before the feeding tube
bed sores and only
grunts for utterance

We knew he still was not
afraid and would go when
he figured out how to fold
his soul just so   enabling
it to squeeze through
the narrow passage

before spreading
full-sky wings

NO PREPARATION

The old don't tell you
how it will be
what to expect

Now I imagine my mother
                all alone
Us with a troublesome adolescent
                we could not leave

I called once a week

She must have had
                certainly had
this constant onslaught
        some new ailment
        mishap
        pain
                everyday

She didn't say
Seemed happy to chat

Cousin called to say I must come
            Was time now
            Not many more days
                to ease her way

SO SAD

Eric Clapton sings with the Allman Brothers,
Why does love have to be so sad? Bob
sings it over and over. *Why does love
have to be so sad?* Louder and louder.
*Why does love have to so sad? Why
does love have to be so sad?* Finally
I say, *Love's not sad. It's joyful, elegant,*
                                                    ecstatic.

Bob stops. Considers this. Looks to
David our friend who's helping
him install the new HD TV with Bose
stereo speakers wired up so he can
blast out concerts—it's taken several
days. He's picked this segment especially to
show Dave how the component parts really
rock out this Crossroads Guitar Festival.

Bob cocks his head. He says, *It's
sad because you have to say goodbye,
goodbye to everything, everybody
you love. That's why it's sad.*
Oh, I say
David says nothing.
We turn the concert off.

SAD SONGS SAD STORIES

She gobbled up every one of the poet's books
about his wife's dying, death, his grieving

Others complained—*That's all he writes-
about—her going, his sadness*

She knew this but craved the stories
like a special kind of candy

The struggle shimmered, the love
sang, the devotion was a lullaby

Where others pushed away—*too
sad, too much suffering*—she gulped

the beauty, the lyrical pain

LAST THINGS

> "Nobody plans to be a ghost"
> —Jane Hirshfield

Too much hope for that
Hope that all who went before
Before they ceased to exist
Exist still in Someother-Else
Else why bother to stumble
Stumbling sometimes breaks bones
Bones dissolve more slowly than flesh
Flesh gives way to ruin
Ruin means nothing lasts
Last things hold special tears

ORA PRO NOBIS

      (Pray for us)

None of us knows
      the exact moment
the Spirit of Mercy and Dread
will circle close over head
and strike the blow
      definite
      and everlasting

Ora Pro Nobis

      Body'll peel away
      like an onion skin
      disposable
      no longer essential
and we'll go
      some with palms outstretched
      others with heels dug in
            gouging out a trench

Ora Pro Nobis

      We ask for grace
      and will
      to wave the flag
      be easily seen
      scooped up quick
      wafted away by the gathering winds

Not to Make a Fuss

ON THE FLOOR

remain a few straws
from the broom
that thwacked the bat
that fell to the floor
when I moved the
glass bird it was
resting beside after
it flew out when
we shook the drapes
after it hid there when
we yelled and waved
dish towels at it as
it swooped through
the living room finally
emerging after four
nights of us cowering
in the bedroom   Door closed
                          tight

TO SEE

His mother said she'd
        never live to see
                the cedar trees
                they were planting
                grow into a hedge

She said she'd never
        get to see her grandchildren

Near the end she said
                    I saw Him!
Nobody asked her *Who?*

CONSENT

> "We stay until we leave."
> —David Meltzer

Until we give
our consent
Yes!

Hold up our arms
Air
Wind
Sky

It will end
as it began

Some push
Some pain
Some giving way
      A rip
        tearing
A tear

We are
      no
            longer
                  here

AUTUMN DUET

I

The neighbor's tree
is getting up
to leave,
cloaking itself
in gold and
vermillion—
a blazing
dying swan
farewell.

II

Earth is flinging herself
with tipped-over glee and
wild-armed whirling into
a tryst with winter, stretching
bare limbs into the encompassing
dark and pressing toward
her lover's ice-cold kiss.

"ALL BUT A LITTLE OF IT BLURS AND LEAKS AWAY"

—Jack Gilbert

Colors remain. Lavender
her mother loved   Turquoise
her youth-eye-color when
she was sun-bronzed
Egg shell skies
and spring daffodils

Shards of old song   "I ran
all the way home" "Teen
Angel can you hear me?"
"They say don't go on
Wolverton Mountain"   "Running
Bear loved little White Dove"

Scenes in mind's photo album
What she wore to friend's
wedding—orange suede
Long dress from Feminist phase
Purple gauze pants bought
in Paris but not who she
gave them to

Sun rising behind him
as he ate huge breakfast
morning their son was born
Her head sliding open as
she floated down wedding aisle
Pour of grace flooding as
she proceeded into the sacrament

Mother's wide gaze before
she left her body

Cold bay water
around her ankles in Sarasota

Smell of babies' heads
Grandmother whiff   India spices
and feces Incense-soaked stuff
from hippie shops
Glass wind chime outside cousin's
playhouse   Car tires fading

DAYS OF THE DEAD

I

THE DEAD

mostly do not
talk to me

certainly deliver
no description

of how they are
where they are

If they have
anything at all

to say it's
I'm still alive

Can't you see?

II

Father dead
so many times
in dreams

I study him suspicious
now in another
If he died in life and

died again in dreams
how come now this
time   this dream

he's here again
walking around
acting as if
he's okay?

III

She asks those
who have crossed
to that other place

a while back
or more recent
if they could please

send back something
if not a word
then perhaps an image

some indication
they've reached their
destination and all

is well   that is if
it's not interfering
with important business

there where they are
now   So far the request
has been ignored

or maybe answers
move more slowly there
across space and time

     IV

My friend said that
our other friend turned
into a star when he died

How does she know
and can I still talk to
him   Another she
said who had died two
weeks before   was there
when our group landed in Delhi
              I thought I saw her face
              on touch down

If they are still around
why don't they speak
more clearly show themselves
in bright light twinkle message
across sky at night

WHEN I AM DEAD

You can throw away
the certificate of recognition
from Nebraska legislature
for Emeritus Status
Keep maybe the actual glass award
It looks pretty in a window

Clothes collection I worked so hard
(good fabrics, lovely style) to attain
having no women's clothing stores
in my small Midwest town
Open closet to friends, have them
choose something if they can
still hobble to the upstairs room
Then I guess heap them
beside the highway
Such colorful flags would
      hardly stop cattle trucks
      maybe some cars
And passengers can ask
      For free?
      Really?

Yes!
And poetry books?
      If you could somehow
      place them in the hands
      of those hungry for words
      searching for metaphors
      to explain our puzzling journey
that would be great!

Notebooks?
    Turn them loose
        to the wind and rain
          dissolving paper and pain
    Transforming perhaps
        into a tiny trail
          showering behind my soul

as it goes
turning once
like Lot's wife
to view all
that was
    beautiful
    hard

    life

RECOMPENSE

    Leaves fallen
           Better able to see sky
                      Flock of geese
                Winging goodbye

IN MY HEAVEN

Barack Obama and Anthony Bourdain lunch on noodles
in an outside restaurant in Vietnam nodding over
hopeful talk of country and world. It is raining while
they agree catsup doesn't belong on hot dogs.

Around the corner I attend the movie version of
The Last Waltz with Bob Dylan, The Band, Emmylou
Harris and other rockers closing the Fillmore
West, sitting in the dark theater between Allen
Ginsberg and Peter Orlovsky, who whispers hoarsely
across me with each group, *Allen? Allen? Who's this?*

Then I smack into a tree at the Dead Sea so I
remember this Israel trip isn't just about me.

In a dark monastery in Ladakh I realize finally
I've found home while butter lamps sputter
beneath ancient tanka paintings.

Highway 81 sings for always in the background with
squeals of brakes and frightened cattle stopping for
traffic light. Cars and trucks buzz and hum until a
crotch rocket explodes beside growling jake brakes.

I suntan turning my skin silky brown, making my eyes
turquoise. No cancer worries.

Rabbits find other tasty snacks instead of my petunias.

People acquire 3-D vision so they understand slights
and hurts from the perspective of the person who
made them.

Baby son turns into my grandson in my arms.

La De Da Dee Di   And the beat goes on …

Delhi horns honk. Drivers make hand signs
out the windows of tiny taxis which miss each other
by paper thinness.

I climb the Himalayas in Birkenstocks and make it
up the Rockies barefoot with no cactus stickers
in feet because I see the plants shooting light.

We make love to Leonard Cohen's, *Hey, That's
No Way to Say Goodbye.*

"TO WANT SOME THINGS TO LIVE BECAUSE THEY WILL LIVE ANYWAY"

—Donald Revell

it will all go on without us
we just slow it down

slow down the world
with her dark glasses on

on her way to the beach
to spread out all sunny

sunny and glowing
taking in the rays and arrows

some arrows sting
others puncture the dream

dream continues into eternity
all morning the lilacs

lift up their lavender arms
singing the purple of life

life will continue   three
blue eggs in robin nest

nest outside the window

"SOMEONE LEFT THE CAKE OUT IN THE RAIN"

—Line from 60s song

When I tell you I left my purse
        out on the patio
Ask me if I had been watching
        the baby robins in their nest

When I say the zipper was open
Laugh that I'm becoming carefree

When I tell you there was
        a thunderstorm
Ask if the thirsty petunias gulped water

When I confess purse, its contents,
        medical cards were soaked
Ask if they have yet begun
        to grow their bounty—
                beauty and wild flowers

SUNDOWN AT FAITH REGIONAL

The setting sun pulls the old women
        from inside the hospital
                into the parking lot
        one crowned in frightened-white hair
                another slowly moving with a walker

Evening is descending
        and like the whirling grackles
        squawking and settling
        in the Healing Garden trees
        where a lotus rises from the pond
        the women head for their vehicles
        wanting to make it home
        before Dark arrives

leaving their old bird men
        murmuring and moaning
        here in their beds behind

NOTHING AT ALL

My friend wished to be Nothing
Wrinkled old man he died
next to his dog and cat

When I tossed his ashes into the Missouri
singing *Good night, Irene I'll see you
in my dreams* the river was
raging   Water flooding   I hoped

he would make it to the Gulf of Mexico
*Don't go Goodbye Bon Voyage I'll
see you in my dreams*   Not body
or man or Nothing exactly   Maybe

a fish   We are training to be Nothing
I don't know why but the Source
or All-That-Is is supposed to be
Nothing   Why would we want that

do you suppose? Well it's probably
better than being Me-Who-I-Am-Now
for all eternity   So I try to let it fly
Fling bits of rickrack stars of

moondust memorabilia of this
vacation and that trip into the trash
instead of the recycle bin but moths
and bugs and creepy things I've done

and said keep reoccurring
I really like sweeping   I believe
women and brooms are meant for
each other   *Oh Whither   O Whither O*

*Whither so high   To sweep the cobwebs
out of the sky*   Brain grooves full
of information   Images of sunsets
ballgames babies birthing and

clean lakes with full moon reflections
Wanting spring in winter Nostalgia
in the fall   Weeping with ecstasy
at weddings or the deep-well meaning

of a song a poem   *Ora pro nobis*
Pray for us   Spirits encased in
material form looking out of
eye soul windows   knocking at

heart door   To be Nothing in Nothing
Land   No music squeezed from
earthly plane   A bar completely empty
even though it is completely stocked
White clouds in clear glass tabletop

Hard to stop listening for the rain
drumming   Wind playing with
leaves in trees arms   How to
not cling to our familiar heart

beat beating   Bleating of hillside sheep
All those dreams come sashaying
across our sleep screen theater
No more holidays   No more Two-Steps

*Oh Lord deliver us to the Tower
of Nothing*   No moment or even
sigh escaping before we make
our formal prayer—blessing

ourselves planet universe
Giving it all up *Up and Away*
It hurts this dissolving
Still it's where we hope to go

www.ingramcontent.com/pod-product-compliance
Lightning Source LLC
Chambersburg PA
CBHW031634160426
43196CB00006B/408